MARRIED LIFE

ADULT
COLORING BOOK

Enjoying this book?

Please leave a review because we would love to know your thoughts, feedback, and opinions to create better paper products for you!

Thank you so much for your support.

MY HUSBAND ASKED ME TO WHISPER DIRTY THINGS IN HIS EAR.

SO I WHISPERED: "KITCHEN, BATHROOM, LIVING ROOM".

MARRIAGE:
AN ENDLESS SLEEPOVER WITH YOUR FAVORITE WEIRDO

WEDDING RINGS:
THE WORLD'S
SMALLEST
HANDCUFFS

BEING MARRIED MEANS JUST SHOUTING "WHAT" FROM OTHER ROOMS

A MAN IS INCOMPLETE UNTIL
HE IS MARRIED.
AFTER THAT, HE IS FINISHED.

A GUY KNOWS HE'S IN LOVE WHEN HE LOSES INTEREST IN HIS CAR FOR A COUPLE OF DAYS.

NEVER LAUGH AT YOUR WIFE'S CHOICE... YOU ARE ONE OF THEM!

MARRIAGE IS A WORKSHOP...
WHERE THE HUSBAND WORKS
& WIFE SHOPS...

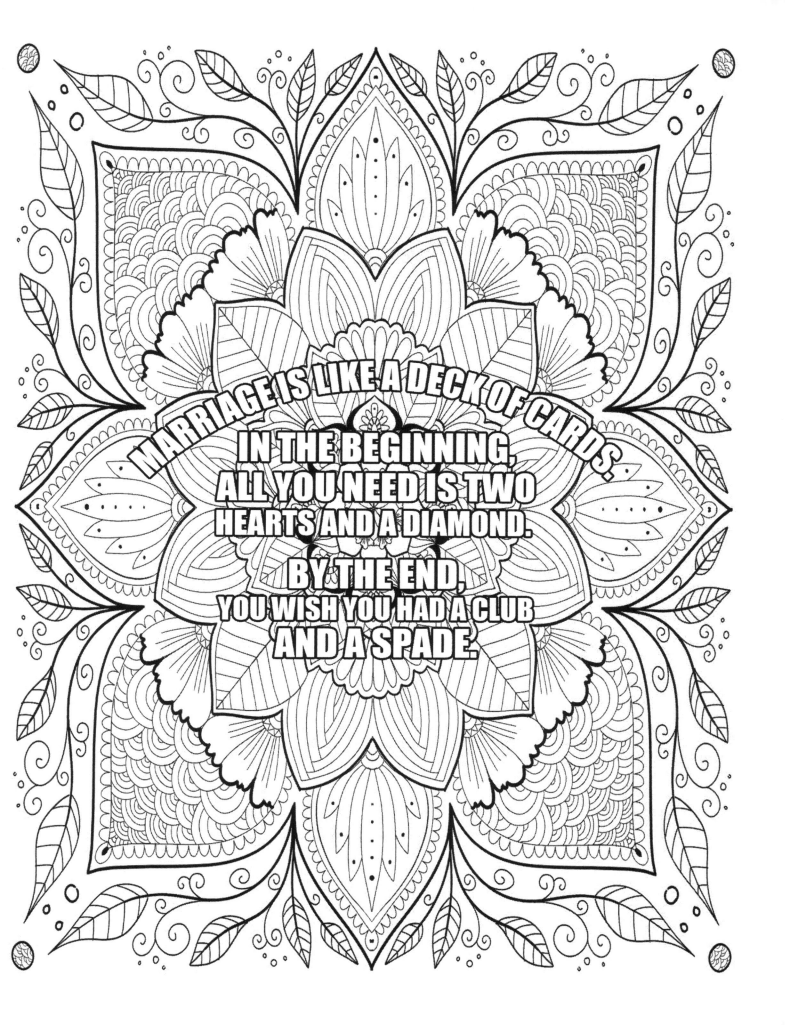

MARRIAGE IS LIKE A DECK OF CARDS.
IN THE BEGINNING,
ALL YOU NEED IS TWO
HEARTS AND A DIAMOND.

BY THE END,
YOU WISH YOU HAD A CLUB
AND A SPADE.

A HUSBAND IS SOMEONE WHO, AFTER TAKING THE TRASH OUT, GIVES THE IMPRESSION HE JUST CLEANED THE WHOLE HOUSE

IF YOU'RE WRONG AND YOU SHUT UP,
YOU'RE WISE.
IF YOU'RE RIGHT AND YOU SHUT UP,
YOU'RE MARRIED.

THE MOST IMPORTANT FOUR WORDS FOR A SUCCESSFUL MARRIAGE:

"I'LL DO THE DISHES"

THE BEST WAY TO REMEMBER YOUR WIFE'S BIRTHDAY IS TO FORGET IT ONCE

MARRIAGE IS A RELATIONSHIP IN WHICH ONE PERSON IS ALWAYS RIGHT AND THE OTHER IS THE HUSBAND